MINECRAFT
VOLUME ALPHA

Sheet Music Selections from the Video Game Soundtrack

Composed by C418

T0109628

CONTENTS

Produced by
Alfred Music
P.O. Box 10003
Van Nuys, CA 91410-0003
alfred.com

Printed in USA.

ISBN-10: 0-7390-9953-1
ISBN-13: 978-0-7390-9953-7
Cover image: © 2011 C418

KEY

Composed by
DANIEL ROSENFELD

Slowly (♩ = 70)

3

DOOR

Composed by
DANIEL ROSENFELD

4

SUBWOOFER LULLABY

Composed by
DANIEL ROSENFELD

Moderately slow (♩ = 76)

(with pedal)

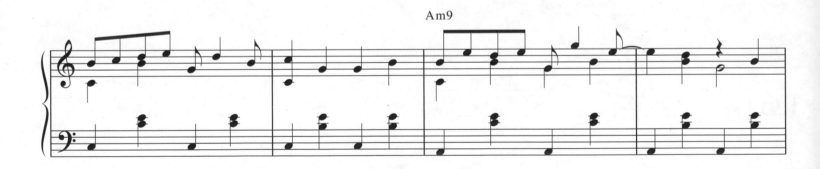

Subwoofer Lullaby - 3 - 1

Cmaj7

Very freely

Em

C

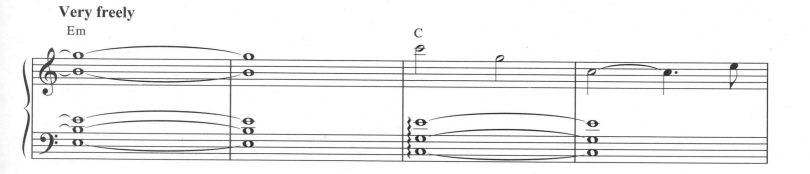

Am

F

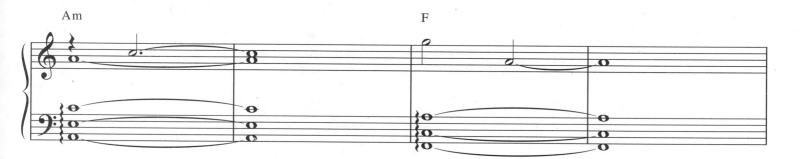

G

C

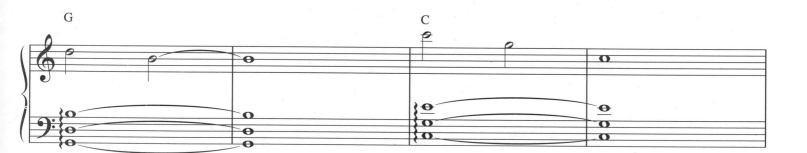

Cmaj7

p   *a tempo*

Fmaj7

Cmaj7

Fmaj7

Cmaj7

DEATH

Composed by
DANIEL ROSENFELD

Death - 1 - 1

LIVING MICE

Composed by
DANIEL ROSENFELD

Fmaj7 C/E

Gsus D7/F♯ Fmaj9

Em7 Gsus D7/F♯

Am7 G D7/A

(counter melody)

Repeat and fade

DRY HANDS

Composed by
DANIEL ROSENFELD

MOOG CITY

Composed by
DANIEL ROSENFELD

Bright (♩ = 138)

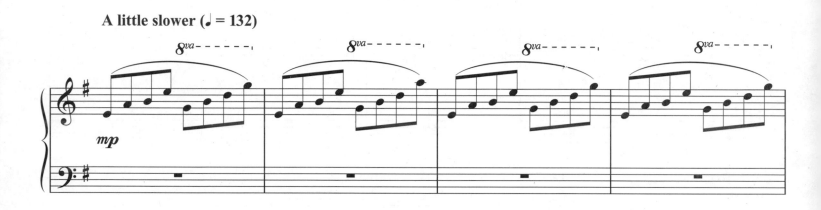

A little slower (♩ = 132)

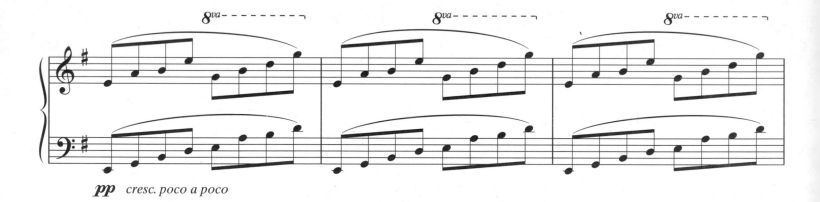

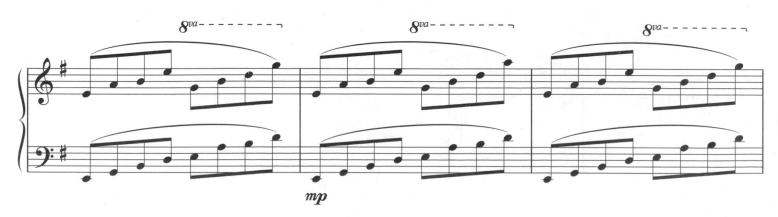

Moog City - 4 - 1

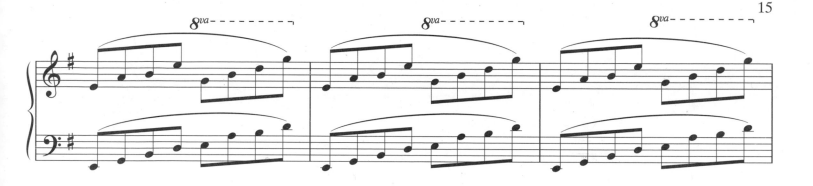

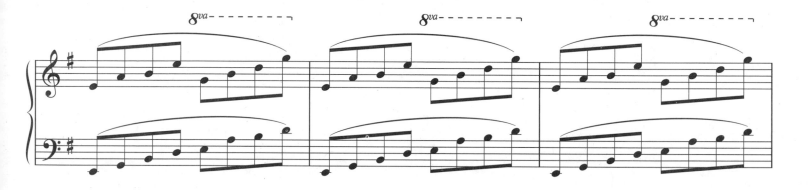

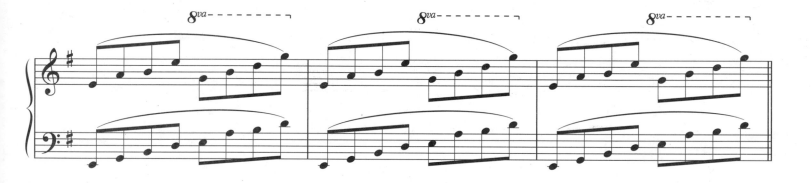

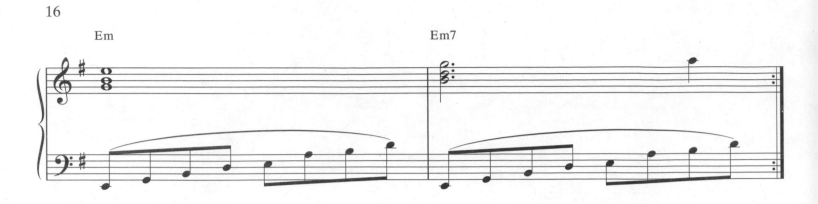

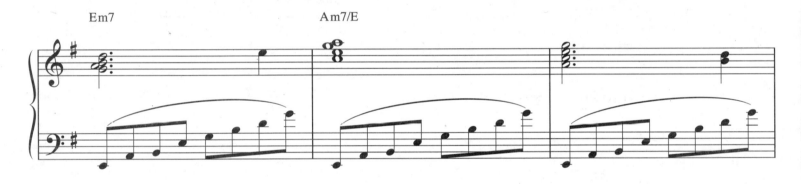

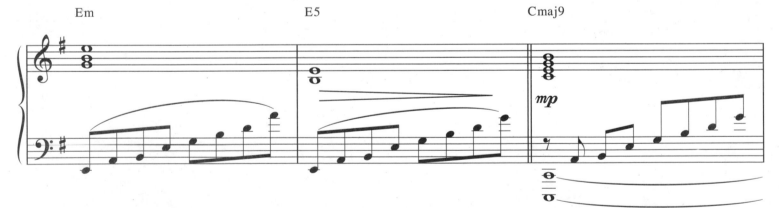

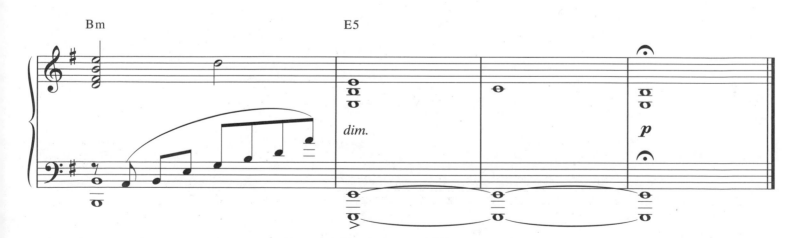

HAGGSTROM

Composed by
DANIEL ROSENFELD

Slowly (♩ = 108)

F#m9

C(9)

MINECRAFT

Composed by
DANIEL ROSENFELD

Repeat as desired

Repeat and fade

ÉQUINOXE

Composed by
DANIEL ROSENFELD

Slowly, in two (♩ = 51)

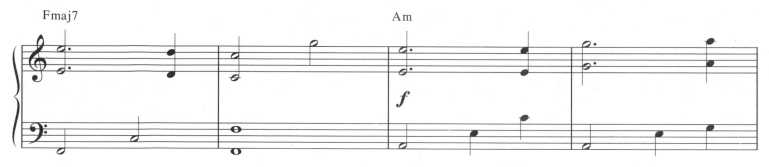

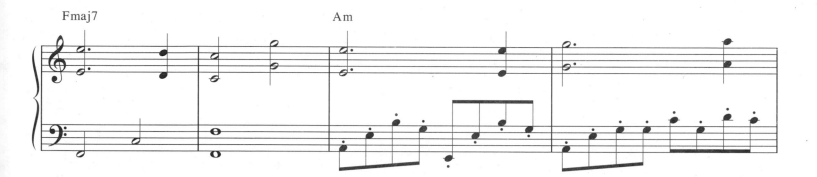

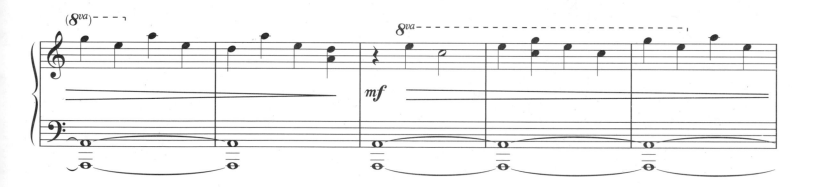

Équinoxe - 2 - 2

MICE ON VENUS

Composed by
DANIEL ROSENFELD

Slowly (♩ = 58)

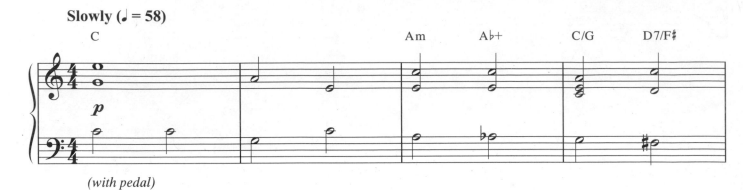

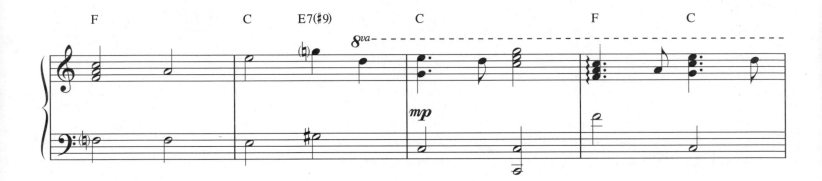

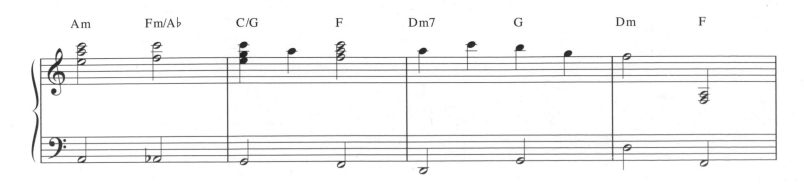

Mice on Venus - 4 - 1

Moderately (♩ = 104)

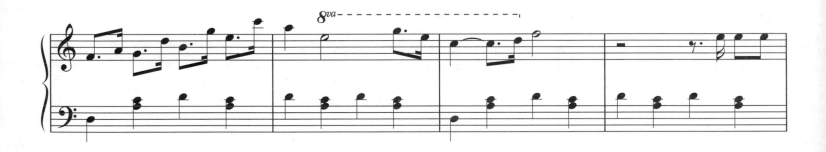

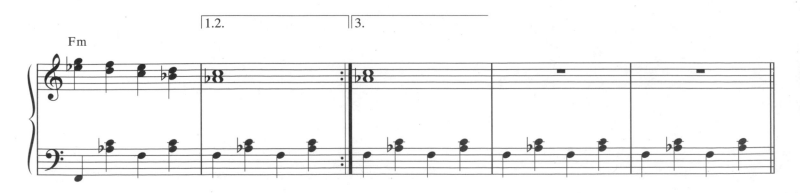

Dm

WET HANDS

Composed by
DANIEL ROSENFELD

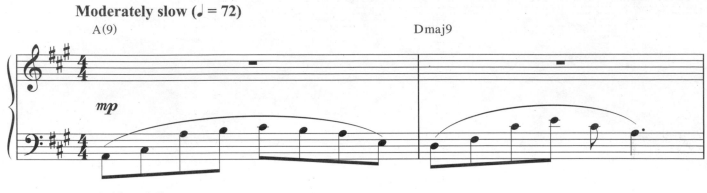

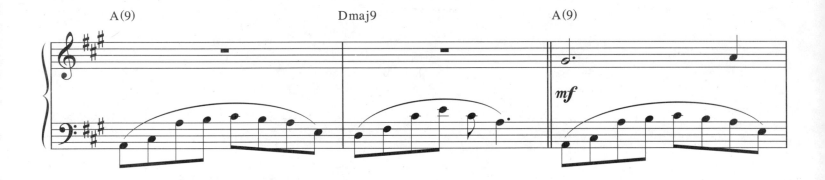

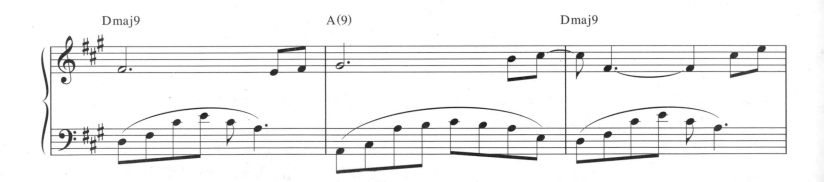

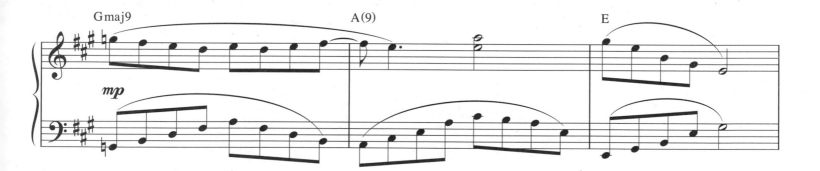

CHRIS

Composed by
DANIEL ROSENFELD

Easy groove (♩ = 92)

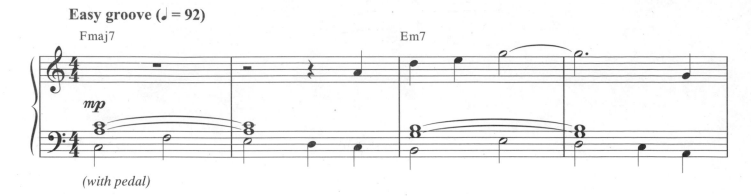

(with pedal)

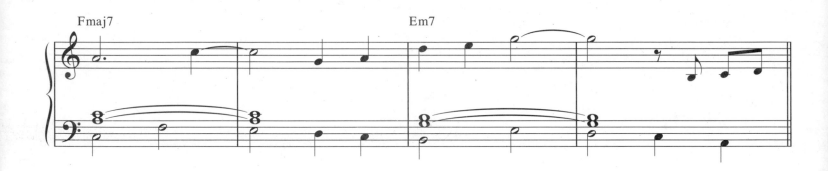

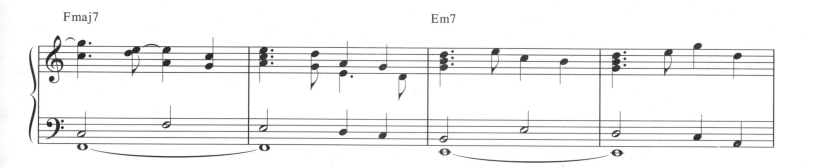

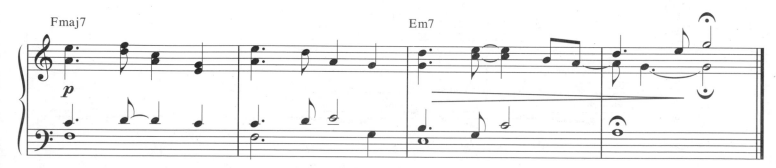

EXCUSE

Composed by
DANIEL ROSENFELD

Moderately (♩ = 92)

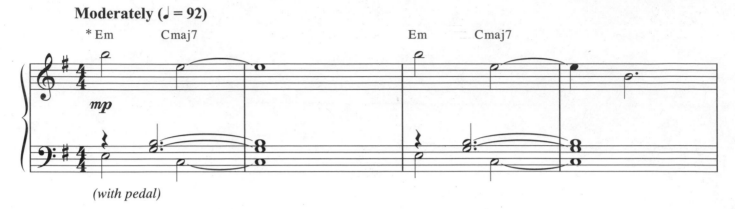

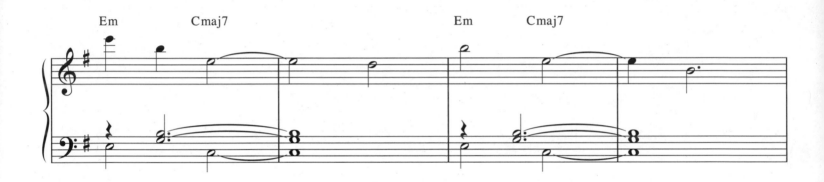

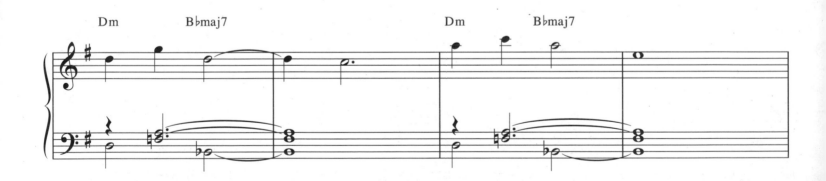

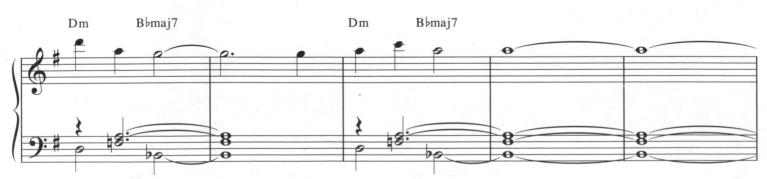

* If desired, for maximum effect set delay to quarter note repeat, very wet.

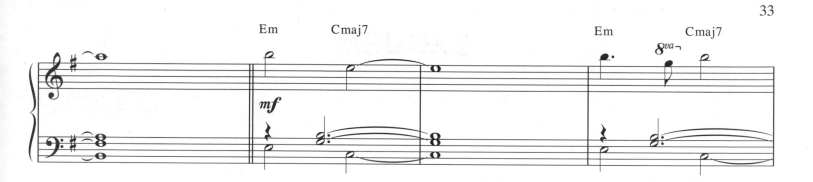

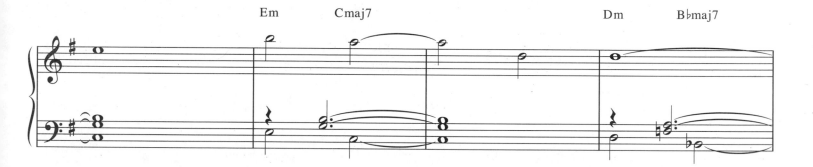

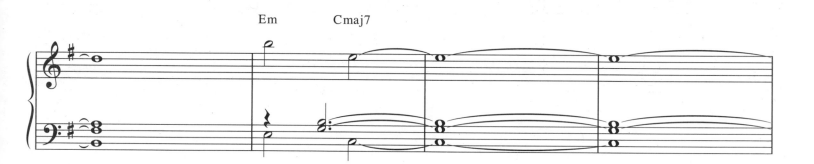

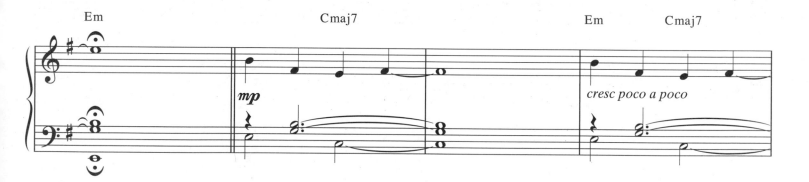

SWEDEN

Composed by
DANIEL ROSENFELD

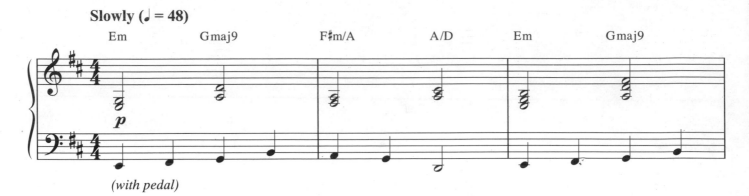

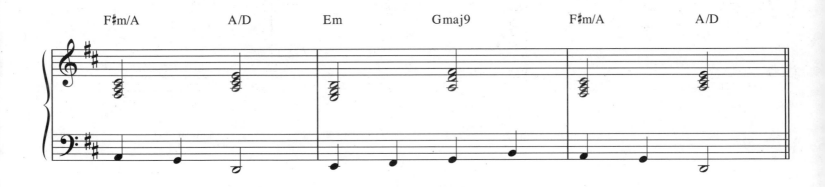

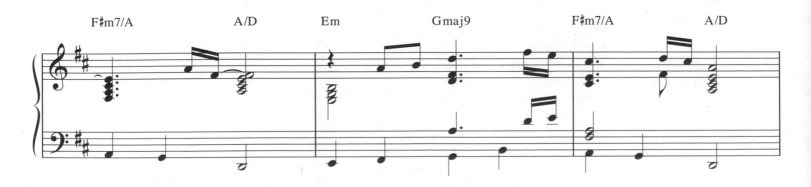

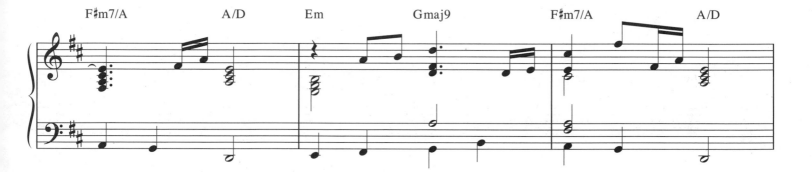

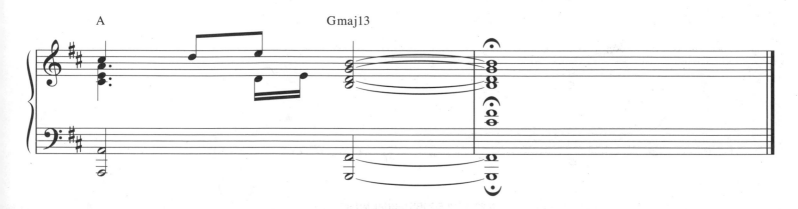

Sweden - 2 - 2

CLARK

Composed by
DANIEL ROSENFELD

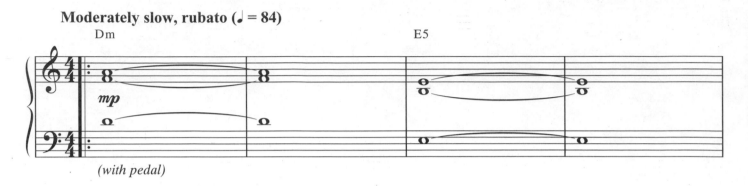

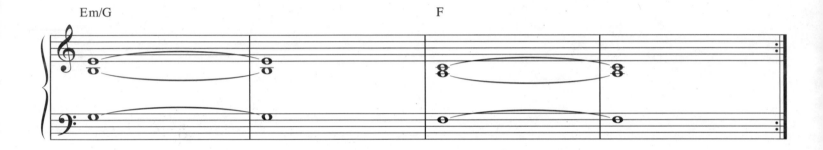

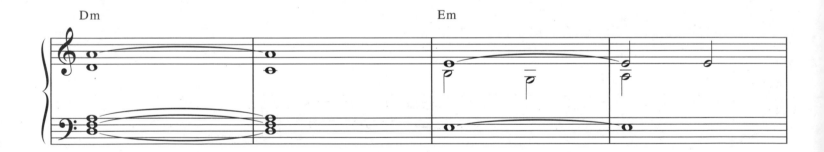

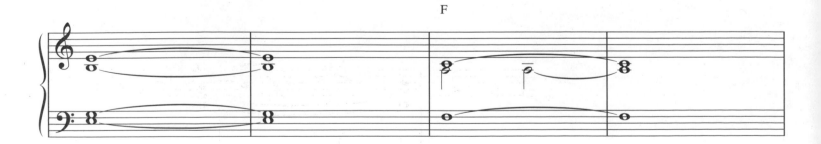

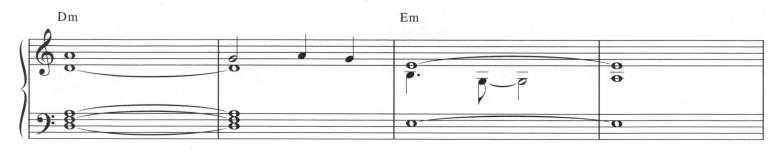

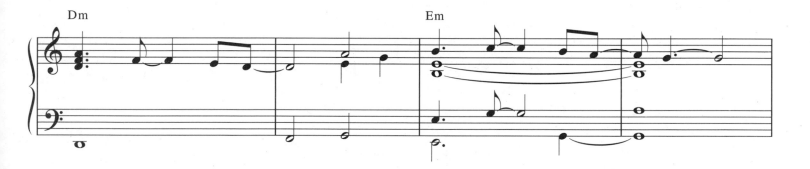

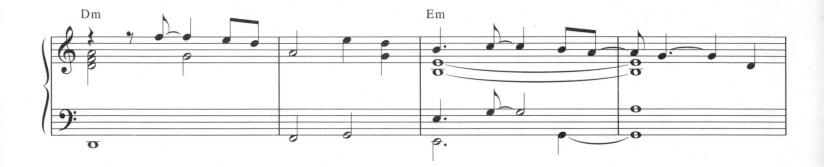

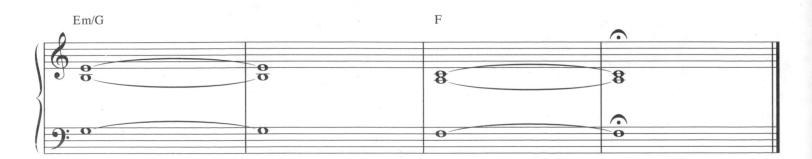

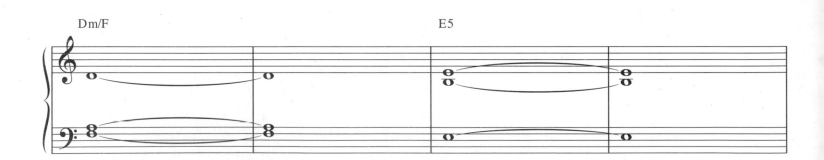

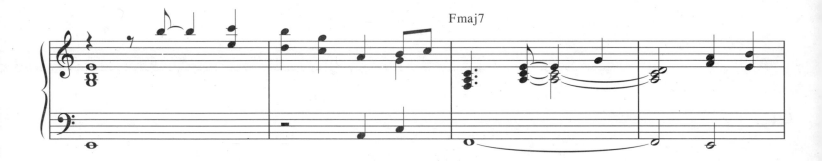

DANNY

Composed by
DANIEL ROSENFELD

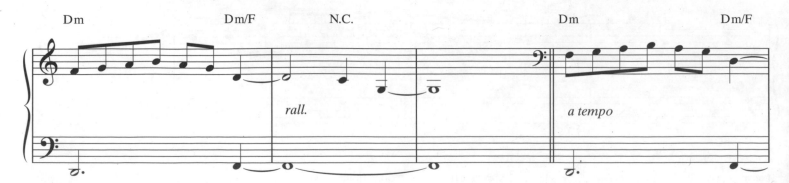

DROOPY LIKES RICOCHET

Composed by
DANIEL ROSENFELD

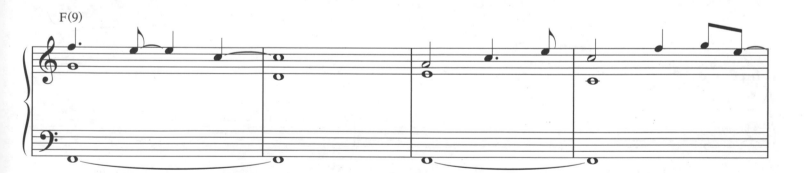

BEGINNING

Composed by
DANIEL ROSENFELD